Fantastic Fruit Recipes

The Only Fruit Cookbook You'll Ever Need

By

Heston Brown

HESTON BROWN

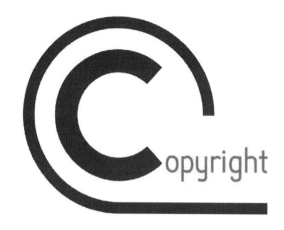

Copyright 2021 Heston Brown

Table of Contents

Introduction

Fresh fruits are fantastically versatile, they make a great option for desserts, snacks, and breakfasts. You can eat fruits without having to prepare them, simply, peel, or cut and eat. But despite their simplicity, they are never the most popular item on the average shopping list. The majority of people prefer to eat unhealthy processed foods.

According to the Centers For Disease Control, one in three people will suffer from diabetes by the year 2050! That doesn't sound too good, does it? If you don't want to become a statistic, eating more fruit instead of chips, chocolate, and cookies will serve you well. Here are some of the health benefits associated with eating fruits:

Disease Prevention: Fruits are high in fiber which helps keep your digestive system in good working order. A high fiber diet is also linked to a decreased risk of several diseases such as cancer, high blood pressure, type 2 diabetes, and heart disease.

Healthy Weight Loss: As mentioned, fruit is rich in fiber, additionally, some fruits have a high-water content. This combination keeps you full for longer, which means you are less likely to snack. Also, water speeds up the metabolism, so the more fruit you eat, the more weight you can expect to lose.

Boosts the Immune System: Studies have found that fruits provide nutrients such as vitamin C, vitamin E, and beta-carotene. All of which have been found to boost the immune system.

Now that you know how good fruit is for you, why not start making some of these recipes?

Bon Appetite...

Salad Recipes

Raspberry and Peach Salad with Mascarpone

Cooking Time: *10 Minutes/****Serves:*** *4 Servings*

Served this tasty raspberry and peach salad with a dah of mascarpone, pistachios, and maple syrup for the perfect touch.

Ingredients

- 1 tablespoon of maple syrup
- A handful of roughly chopped pistachios
- 16 raspberries sliced in halves
- 1 drop of vanilla extract
- 100 ml of double cream
- 100 grams of mascarpone
- 1 teaspoon of lemon thyme leaves
- 50 grams of caster sugar
- 2 ripe peaches, stone removed and thinly sliced

Directions

1. Arrange the slices of peach onto four plates and sprinkle some caster sugar over them.

2. Sprinkle most of the lemon thyme leaves over the peaches.

3. In a small bowl, whisk together the rest of the sugar, double cream, vanilla extract, and mascarpone.

4. Drop blobs of the mixture onto the peaches.

5. Scatter the raspberries, pistachios, and the rest of the thyme over the top.

6. Drizzle with maple syrup and serve.

Apple & Beetroot Salad with Swedish Meatballs

Cooking Time: *40 Minutes/**Serves:** 4 Servings*

Extra juicy meatballs served with a salad packed full of flavor, served with a creamy herb sauce.

Ingredients For the Meatballs

- 2 tablespoons of crème fraiche, half-fat
- 2 teaspoons of vegetable bouillon powder boiled in 300 ml of water
- 1 teaspoon of thyme leaves
- 1 tablespoon of rapeseed oil
- 1 large egg
- 2 cloves of garlic, finely grated
- 4 tablespoons of fresh dill, chopped
- 1 grated onion
- 100 grams of courgette, squeezed of excess juice and grated
- 500 grams of lean pork mince
- Black pepper
- Cooking oil

Ingredients For the Salad

- 320 grams of cooked beetroot, sliced into strips
- The juice of ½ a lemon
- 4 tablespoons of chopped parsley
- 1 thinly sliced red onion
- 1 chopped large apple

Directions

Combine half the garlic, half the dill, the onion, courgette, and pork into a large bowl, season with black pepper and stir to combine.

Crack the egg into the mixture and use your hands to combine the ingredients.

Break of small pieces of the mixture about the size of a walnut, and roll them into balls. The mixture should make about 28 balls.

In a large frying pan, heat ¼ of an inch of oil in a frying pan and fry the meatballs until they turn into a pale golden color and become firm. It should take about 6-8 minutes to cook each batch.

In another saucepan, add the thyme, the rest of the garlic, the bouillon, the water and bring the ingredients to a boil.

Remove the saucepan from the heat, add the rest of the dill, the crème fraiche, and the meatballs and use a large spoon to combine everything making sure that the meatballs are coated.

To make the salad, combine the capers, parsley, onion, lemon juice, and beetroot.

Divide the meatballs onto plates, and serve with the salad on the side.

Summer Peach Spinach Salad with Goats Cheese

Cooking Time: *15 Minutes/***Serves:** *4 Servings*

A fresh peach salad recipe with delicious goats cheese

Ingredients For the Salad

- ½ a cup of toasted almonds
- ½ a cup of goat cheese crumbles
- ½ a thinly sliced red onion
- 1 diced avocado
- 2 sliced large peaches
- 4 cups of spinach
- 2 tablespoons of balsamic vinegar

Ingredients For the Dressing

- 1 clove of minced garlic
- ½ a teaspoon of Dijon mustard
- 1 clove of minced garlic
- 3 tablespoons of extra virgin olive oil
- 3 tablespoons of balsamic vinegar
- Salt and pepper

Directions

1. To make the dressing, combine the Dijon mustard, minced garlic, olive oil, balsamic vinegar, salt and pepper in a medium sized bowl and whisk together thoroughly.

2. To make the salad, combine the spinach and the balsamic vinegar and toss to combine.

3. Add the red onion, goats cheese, avocado, peach, and toasted almonds and toss to combine.

4. Divide onto plates and serve.

Feta and Pomegranate Salad Recipe

Cooking Time: *10 Minutes/****Serves:*** *2 Servings*

You can't go wrong with this simple, yet delicious pomegranate salad and feta recipe.

Ingredients for the Salad

- 1 packet of feta cheese, crumbled
- ¼ red onion, sliced
- The seeds from one pomegranate
- 1 packet of lettuce
- ¼ cup of granulated sugar
- ½ a cup of pecans

Ingredients for the Dressing

- The zest and juice of 1 lemon
- 3 tablespoons of extra virgin olive oil
- 3 tablespoons of red wine vinegar
- 1 teaspoon of Dijon mustard

Directions

1. Combine the sugar and the pecans into a frying pan and cook on a medium temperature until the sugar turns into a caramel color and melts. Keep stirring while cooking to prevent burning.

2. Place a sheet of aluminium foil on a plate and spoon the pecans onto it to cool down.

3. Once the pecans have cooled down, break them up using a rolling pin.

4. Combine the lettuce, feta cheese, red onion, pomegranate seeds, and pecan in a large bowl and toss to combine.

5. In a small bowl, combine the lemon juice, lemon zest, olive oil, vinegar, Dijon mustard, salt and pepper, and whisk to combine.

6. Pour the dressing over the salad, toss to coat, and divide into bowls.

Quinoa Salad with Summer Fruit

Cooking Time: *20 Minutes/**Serves:** 4 Servings*

Spice up some quinoa by combining it with fruit and seasoning.

Ingredients

- The juice and zest of 1 lemon
- 2 tablespoons of olive oil
- 1 handful of chopped parsley
- 1 handful of chopped mint
- 50 grams of chopped hazelnuts
- 3 peaches, seed removed and chopped
- 100 grams of quinoa

Directions

1. Prepare the quinoa according to the instructions on the packet. Once cooked, drain the remaining water and set the quinoa to one side to cool down for five minutes.

2. Add the hazelnuts, fruits, mint, and parsley to the quinoa and toss to combine.

3. In a small bowl, combine the lemon juice, lemon zest, and olive oil, whisk together thoroughly, pour over the salad and toss to combine.

4. Divide the salad into bowls and serve.

Mint and Orange Salad

Cooking Time: *15 Minutes/***Serves:** *4 Servings*

This combination of mint and orange makes a very flavorful salad.

Ingredients

- 1 tablespoon of rosewater
- 1 small bunch of finely chopped mint leaves
- A few mint leaves for garnish
- 12 dates, stone removed and cut in half lengthways
- 4 oranges

Directions

1. Peel the orange and remove the white pith.

2. In a medium sized bowl, combine orange, dates, rose syrup, chopped mint, and toss to combine.

3. Divide the salad into bowls, garnish with mint leaves and serve.

Peach Salad Topped with Hazelnut

Cooking Time: *20 Minutes/****Serves:*** *6 Servings*

Give your salad an extra crunch by topping it with hazelnuts.

Ingredients For the Salad

- 1 packet of rocket leaves
- 100 grams of lamb's lettuce
- 250 grams of soft goats cheese
- 3 tablespoons of extra virgin olive oil
- 4 peaches, stone removed, thinly sliced

Ingredients For the Dressing

- 1 tablespoon of sherry vinegar
- 3 tablespoons of extra-virgin olive oil
- 50 grams of chopped hazelnuts, skin removed

Directions

1. Prepare the oven by heating it to 350 degrees F.

2. In a large bowl, combine the olive oil and the sherry vinegar and whisk together thoroughly.

3. Spread the hazelnuts out onto a roasting tray and bake for 5 minutes until they turn golden.

4. Once cooked, remove them from the oven and tip the hazelnuts into the dressing.

5. Arrange the peach on the roasting tray, sprinkle olive oil over them, and season with salt and pepper. Roast the peaches for 5 minutes.

6. Place the cheese on the baking tray and bake until it just starts melting, this should take around two minutes.

7. Add the rocket and the lamb's lettuce to the dressing and toss to coat.

8. Divide the salad into bowls, top with the roasted peaches, a slice of cheese and serve.

Blue Cheese Salad with Griddled Pear

Cooking Time: *15 Minutes/**Serves:** 4 Servings*

This combination of sweet and sour makes for a very stylish salad.

Ingredients

- 1 packet of blue cheese, crumbled
- 1 bag of mixed leaf salad
- 1 tablespoon of honey
- 1 tablespoon of white wine vinegar
- 2 tablespoons of olive oil
- 4 sliced ripe pears

Directions

Combine the pears and 1 tablespoon of olive oil in a large bowl and toss to coat.

Heat a frying pan and cook the pears for one minute on each side, you will need to do this in batches.

In a small bowl, combine the rest of the olive oil, honey, and vinegar and whisk to combine.

Combine the dressing with the pear, cheese and mixed leaf salad and toss to combine.

Divide onto plates and serve.

Grape Salad with Blue Cheese and Caramelized Pecans

Cooking Time: *15 Minutes/**Serves:** 4 Servings*

If you are looking for a balance of crunchy, sweet, sour, and smooth, this is the salad for you.

Ingredients

- 140 grams of blue cheese, crumbled
- 50 grams of seedless grapes of your choice sliced in halves
- 1 bag of rocket
- 2 heads of chicory
- 2 tablespoons of olive oil
- 1 tablespoon of balsamic vinegar
- 50 grams of pecans
- 2 tablespoons of caster sugar
- A knob of butter
- Cooking spray
- Salt and pepper

Directions

1. Heat the sugar and butter in a small frying pan over a medium temperature.

2. Once melted, add the pecans, stir to combine, turn the temperature down to low and let it sit for 5 minutes until the nuts become crispy.

3. Oil a baking sheet and tip the pecans onto it, leave them to cool down and then chop them into small pieces.

4. In a small bowl, combine the olive oil, vinegar, salt and pepper and whisk together thoroughly.

5. Combine the rocket, chicory leaves, grapes, and three quarters of the dressing, and toss to combine.

6. Divide the salad onto plates, sprinkle the nuts and cheese over the top. Drizzle with the remaining dressing and serve.

Fruit Drinks

Passion Fruit Martini – Alcohol Free

Preparation Time: *5 Minutes/***Serves***: 2 Servings*

Get the same amount of fun without alcohol.

Ingredients

- Sparkling grape juice
- A handful of ice
- 2 teaspoons of syrup sugar
- 100 ml of alcohol-free spirit
- The white of 1 egg
- The juice of 1 lemon
- 3 passion fruits sliced in halves

Directions

1. Use a spoon to remove the flesh from the passion fruit and transfer it to t cocktail shaker.

2. Add the Syrup, spirit, egg white and lemon juice and shake until the mixture becomes frothy.

3. Add the ice and continue shaking until the shaker turns cold.

4. Strain the drink into martini glasses.

5. Add grape juice and decorate with the passion fruit halves.

Tasty Tropical Smoothie

Preparation Time: *5 Minutes/***Serves:** *2 Servings*

This simple vitamin-packed smoothie is a great way to get your day started.

Ingredients

- 1 sliced banana
- 500 ml of pineapple juice
- 1 chopped mango
- 3 peeled kiwi

Directions

1. Combine all the ingredients in a food processor and blend until smooth.

2. Pour into glasses and serve.

Martini with Passion Fruit

Preparation Time: *5 Minutes/****Serves:*** *2 Servings*

This simple cocktail makes the perfect party companion.

Ingredients

- Prosecco
- 1 tablespoon of sugar syrup
- 1 tablespoon of lime juice
- 30 ml of passoa
- 60 ml of vanilla vodka
- 2 passion fruit, ripe
- A handful of ice

Directions

1. Use a spoon to remove the seeds from the passion fruit and transfer them into the cocktail shaker.

2. Add the sugar syrup, lime juice, passoa, vodka, and ice and shake to combine until the cocktail shaker is cold.

3. Strain the drink into the martini glasses.

4. Add some prosecco, half a passion fruit and serve.

Fantastic Fruit Flavored Mocktail

Preparation Time: *5 Minutes/***Serves:** *4 Servings*

This fruity non-alcoholic beverage is truly satisfying.

Ingredients

- A bottle of sparkling water of your choice
- 400 ml of orange juice
- 4 tablespoons of grenadine
- A handful of blueberries
- A handful of green grapes
- You will need 4 bamboo skewers

Directions

1. Make the stirrers by threading the blueberries and the grapes onto the bamboo skewers.

2. Fill four glasses with the grenadine.

3. Top with some orange juice.

4. Add some sparkling water and serve with the skewers.

Tangy Fruit Punch

Preparation Time: *10 Minutes/**Serves:** 10 Servings*

If you are planning a summer party, this non-alcoholic fruit punch makes the perfect companion.

Ingredients

- 300 ml of lemonade
- 300 ml of orange juice
- 500 ml of pineapple juice
- 1 handful of ice
- 1 handful of mint leaves
- ½ a lemon, sliced
- ½ an orange, sliced
- 10 strawberries, sliced

Directions

1. In a large jug, combine the ice, fruit, and mint.

2. Add the juice and stir to combine.

3. Add the lemonade and stir to combine.

4. Pour into glasses and serve.

Vanilla, Apple, and Ginger Punch

Preparation Time: *5 Minutes/***Serves:** *10 Servings*

A revitalizing ginger drink with a twist.

Ingredients

- A piece of ginger (thumb-sized), peeled and sliced thinly
- 1 apple, sliced thinly
- The juice of 2 limes
- 2 limes cut into wedges
- 500 ml of vanilla vodka
- 500 ml of chilled apple juice
- 1 liter of ginger beer
- Plenty of ice

Directions

1. In a large jug, combine the lime juice, vanilla vodka, apple juice, and ginger beer and stir to combine.

2. Add the ginger, apple, and lime wedges, and stir to combine.

3. Add the ice just before serving.

Punchy Peach Cocktail

Preparation Time: *10 Minutes/***Serves:** *8 Servings*

Give your cocktail an extra kick with this punchy peach flavor.

Ingredients

- 1 liter bottle of sparkling water of your choice
- Plenty of ice
- ½ a lemon, sliced
- 1 sliced peach
- 150 ml of peach schnapps
- 750 ml bottle of rose wine
- The juice and zest of 1 ½ lemons
- 4 tablespoons of caster sugar

Directions

1. Combine the sugar, lemon zest and 100 ml of water in a saucepan and boil over a medium temperature until the sugar dissolves.

2. Leave the mixture to cool down completely, and then pour it into a jug.

3. Add the sparkling water, lemon juice, and wine and stir to combine.

4. Add plenty of ice, the peach and the sliced lemons before serving.

Beautiful Berry Daiquiri

Preparation Time: 10 Minutes/Serves: 1 Serving

Treat yourself with this berry daiquiri for one.

Ingredients

- 1 slice of lime for serving
- 100 ml of white rum
- 1 tablespoon of lemon juice
- The juice of ½ a lime
- A handful of ice
- 8 ounces of berries of your choice

Directions

1. Blend the berries to a pulp and sieve to get rid of the pips.

2. Add the ice to the blender and pulse to crush.

3. Add the pulp, rum, lemon juice, and lime juice and blend to combine.

4. Pour into a cocktail glass, top with lime slice and drink.

Gin Spitzer with Watermelon

Cooking Time: *10 Minutes/***Serves:** *8 Servings*

A revitalizing cocktail perfect for those late summer evenings.

Ingredients

- 1 liter bottle of sparkling water of your choice
- 2 tablespoons of gin
- 100 grams of chopped watermelon
- 2 large limes cut into 16 slices

Directions

1. Squeeze the juice from 2 slices of lime into each glass and add the lime pieces.

2. Divide the watermelon into the glasses.

3. Add some ice cubes to each glass.

4. Top with sparkling water and serve.

Fruit Desserts

Fantastic Fruit Scones

Cooking Time: *10 Minutes/****Serves:*** *8 Servings*

Make these tasty fruit scones and less than 15 minutes.

Ingredients

- Clotted cream and jam to serve
- 1 whipped egg for glazing
- 100 grams of sultanas
- 1 squeeze of lemon juice
- 1 teaspoon of vanilla extract
- ¼ teaspoon of salt
- 175 ml of milk
- 3 tablespoons of caster sugar
- 85 grams of butter
- 1 teaspoon of baking powder
- 350 grams of self-rising flour

Directions

1. Prepare the oven by heating it to 350 degrees F.

2. Combine the flour, baking powder and salt in a large bowl and stir to combine.

3. Spoon the butter into the mixture and use your hands to turn it into a crumble like consistency.

4. Add the sugar and blend with your hands.

5. Heat the milk in the microwave for 30 seconds.

6. Remove the milk from the microwave, add the lemon juice and the vanilla and stir to combine.

7. Heat a baking tray in the oven.

8. Form a hole in the middle of the flour mixture and pour the milk mixture into it.

9. Add the sultanas and stir to combine.

10. Sprinkle some flour onto your work surface and tip the dough onto it.

11. Fold the dough with your hands until it becomes smooth and mould it into a circle.

12. Dip a 5 cm smooth cutter into flour and cut the dough into four scone shapes.

13. Brush the egg over the tops of the scones and then arrange them onto the hot baking tray.

14. Bake the scones for 10 minutes until they turn golden.

15. Remove from the oven, top with clotted cream and jam and serve.

Foxy Fruit Medley

Cooking Time: *15 Minutes*/**Serves:** *8 Servings*

If you're looking for a luscious, but light summer dessert, this is it!

Ingredients

- 2 teaspoons of honey
- 1 peeled large orange, segmented and cut in halves
- 400 grams of mixed berries of your choice, sliced
- 100 grams of seedless grapes cut in halves
- 150 grams of pineapple chunks
- 1 mango, seeded, and sliced into chunks
- 2 skinless kiwis, sliced

Directions

1. Combine all the fruits in a large bowl and toss to combine.

2. Put the bowl in the fridge for 30 minutes.

3. Divide into bowls, drizzle with honey and serve.

Awesome Almond & Apple Crumble Pie

Cooking Time: *50 Minutes/**Serves:** 6 Servings*

For the best of both worlds, combine apple crumble and fruit pie, you can't go wrong.

Ingredients For the Fruit Pie

- Ice cream, custard, or clotted cream to serve
- 1 whipped egg
- 1 block of short crust pastry
- 2 tablespoons of plain flour
- ½ a teaspoon of mixed spice
- 50 grams of golden caster sugar
- 8 apples of your choice, peeled, quartered and cored

Ingredients For the Crumble

- 30 grams of flaked almonds
- 70 grams of butter, sliced into cubes and cold
- 70 grams of golden caster sugar
- 50 grams of ground almonds
- 50 grams of plain flour

Directions

1. Prepare the oven by heating it to 350 degrees F.

2. Prepare the crumble by combining the almonds, sugar, flour, and a pinch of salt in a large bowl and toss to combine.

3. Add the butter and combine with your fingers to form a breadcrumb like consistency.

4. Add the almonds and combine.

5. Combine the apples, flour, mixed spice, and sugar and toss to combine.

6. Dust your surface with flour and roll out the pastry to form a circle of around 20 cm all the way around.

7. Place the pastry into a pie dish, then crimp and trim the edge.

8. Brush the edges with the egg.

9. Arrange the apple mixture into the pie dish, spoon the crumble over the top and bake for 40 minutes.

10. When the topping and pastry has become golden, remove it from the oven, let it cool down for about 15 minutes, and serve with ice cream, custard, or cream.

Tropical Fruit Flavored Frozen Yogurt

Cooking Time: *15 Minutes/**Serves:** 6 Servings*

This recipe is literally magic!

Ingredients

- 200 gram of passion fruit seeds and diced tropical fruit to serve
- 2 tablespoons of maple syrup
- 170 grams of Greek yogurt
- 480 grams of tropical fruit mix, frozen

Directions

1. Put all the ingredients apart from the passion fruit seeds and the tropical fruit into a food processor and blend.

2. Scoop the mixture into bowls, top with the passion fruit seeds and the tropical fruit and serve.

Fruity Rainbow Lollies

Preparation Time: *20 Minutes*/**Serves:** *6 Servings*

Give your kids and yourself a guilt-free healthy dessert with these fruity rainbow lollies.

Ingredients

- 100 grams of frozen blackberries
- 100 grams of frozen raspberries
- 2 kiwis, peeled and chopped
- 400 grams of yogurt
- 2 bananas
- 100 grams of chopped mango

Directions

1. Combine 100 grams of yogurt, half a banana and the mango in food processor and blend to combine.

2. Pour the mixture into six lolly molds and put a stick into them.

3. Freeze the lollies for 1 hour .

4. Combine the kiwi fruit, yogurt, half a banana in a food processor and blend to combine.

5. Remove the lolly molds from the fridge, pour the mixture into them and freeze for another 1 hour.

6. Do the same with the blackberries, then the raspberries.

7. Put a lid over the lollies and freeze overnight.

8. The next day, run the moulds under warm water to remove the lollies.

Lemon and Strawberry Sorbet

Cooking Time: *20 Minutes/***Serves:***10 Servings*

If you want a dessert that's bursting with fruitfulness and refreshing, this is for you.

Ingredients

- 4 lbs of strawberries
- 1 lb of caster sugar
- 2 roughly chopped lemons
- The juice from 2 lemons

Directions

1. Add the caster sugar and the lemon to a food processor and blend until a puree is formed.

2. Pour the puree into a bowl and put it to one side.

3. Blend the strawberries until a puree is formed and add them to the lemon mixture.

4. Keep adding the lemon juice until the taste is just right, the lemon shouldn't overpower the strawberries.

5. Spoon the mixture into a freezer proof container and freeze overnight.

White Chocolate Crumble with Sugar Coated Strawberries

Cooking Time: *1 Hour/**Serves:** 4 Servings*

Crunchy, fruity, and sweet, this recipe is more than delicious.

Ingredients

- Mint leaves to serve
- 20 grams of chopped pistachios
- 4 tablespoons of crème fraiche
- 400 grams of strawberries, tops removed, sliced into quarters
- 100 grams of melted white chocolate
- 50 grams of melted butter
- 20 grams of light brown sugar
- 50 grams of corn starch
- 60 grams of powdered milk

Directions

1. Prepare the oven by heating it to 300 degrees F.

2. In a large bowl, combine the corn starch, milk powder, and half the sugar and toss to combine.

3. Melt the white chocolate and the butter in the microwave for 60 seconds and stir to combine.

4. Tip the milk mixture into the white chocolate mixture and stir to combine until a crumble like texture is achieved.

5. Spread the mixture onto a baking tray and bake until it turns golden in color.

6. Take the tray out of the oven and leave the crumble to cool down.

7. Put the strawberries into a bowl, top with some of the crumble, the pistachios, and a spoonful of crème fraiche.

8. Divide into bowls, top with the mint leaves and serve.

Random Fruit Recipes

Baked Nectarine & Raspberries with Honey & Almonds

Cooking Time: *30 Minutes/****Serves:*** *4 servings*

You can't go wrong with baked fruit, crunchy almonds and honey to satisfy your sweet tooth.

Ingredients

- Clotted cream to serve
- 175 grams of raspberries
- The seeds of 1 vanilla pod
- 1 tablespoon of butter
- 1 tablespoon of golden caster sugar
- 1 tablespoon of toasted flaked almonds
- The yolk of 1 large egg
- 100 grams of amaretti biscuits, crushed
- 4 nectarines cut in halves, stones removed
- 2 tablespoons of clear honey
- 125 ml of wine

Directions

1. In a large bowl, combine the honey and wine and stir until the honey has dissolved.

2. Arrange the nectarines flesh side up in a baking dish.

3. In another large bowl, combine the crushed biscuits, almonds, egg yolk and two tablespoons of the wine mixture and stir to combine.

4. Spoon the mixture onto the nectarines.

5. Sprinkle some sugar on top of the mixture.

6. Put a knob of butter on top of the mixture.

7. Pour the honey mixture into the baking dish, but not over the nectars.

8. Add 1 tablespoon of water.

9. Add the vanilla pod and refrigerate for up to 4 hours.

10. Prepare the oven by heating it to 300 degrees F.

11. Remove the nectarines from the fridge and bake them for 30 minutes.

12. Once the filling is golden and crisp, and the nectarines are soft.

13. Remove the nectarines from the oven and tip the raspberries into the juice.

14. Leave it to cool down for 15 minutes and then serve with crème.

Beautiful Berry Flavored Coulis

Cooking Time: *5 Minutes/**Serves:** Makes 200 ml*

You can spoon the delightful red topping onto the dessert of your choice.

Ingredients

- 100 grams of golden caster sugar
- 100 grams of redcurrant, stems removed
- 200 grams of raspberries

Directions

1. Combine the redcurrants, raspberries, and sugar into a saucepan and heat over a medium temperature.

2. Use the back of a fork to crush the berries.

3. Stir until the sugar has dissolved and the berries have turned into a sauce.

4. Use a sieve to strain the mixture.

5. You can either use the coulis immediately, or leave it to cool down completely and refrigerate until you are ready to use it.

Citrus Inspired Creamy Garlic & Spinach Salmon

Cooking Time: *20 Minutes/***Serves:** *2 Servings*

If you want to add some zing to your salmon, try this recipe.

Ingredients

- 5 tablespoons of milk
- 75 grams of mascarpone
- The juice of 1 lemon
- The zest of 1 lemon
- 1 thinly sliced lemon
- 170 grams of baby spinach
- 2 cloves of thinly sliced garlic
- 2 skinless salmon fillets
- 1 tablespoon of olive oil
- 2 sweet potatoes

Directions

1. Prepare the oven by heating it to 350 degrees F.

2. Pierce the sweet potatoes with a fork and bake for 40 minutes.

3. Heat ½ a tablespoon of olive oil in a frying pan over medium temperature and brown the salmon on both sides, you don't need to cook it.

4. Put the salmon on a plate, and heat the rest of the oil.

5. Fry the garlic for about 30 seconds and add the lemon zest, lemon juice, and spinach and stir to combine.

6. Add 2 tablespoons of milk.

7. Add the mascarpone, and stir to combine until the spinach wilts.

8. Transfer the spinach mixture into an ovenproof dish, add the salmon and the lemon slices and bake for 10 minutes.

9. Once the sweet potatoes are cooked, scoop the flesh from the skins into a bowl and add the rest of the milk. Mash to combine.

10. Divide the salmon and spinach mixture onto plates, add a scoop of sweet potatoes and serve.

Luscious Lemon Coated Spring Greens

Cooking Time: *15 Minutes/***Serves:** *8 Servings*

Give your greens a unique flavor with this lemon-inspired dish.

Ingredients For the Greens

- 400 grams of spring greens, chopped with stalks removed
- 250 grams of broccoli florets

Ingredients For The Dressing

- 2 tablespoons of olive oil
- The juice from 1 lemon
- The zest from 1 lemon

Directions

1. For the dressing, combine the olive oil, lemon zest, lemon juice, and garlic and whisk together thoroughly.

2. Add water to a large saucepan and boil.

3. Cook the greens and broccoli for 5 minutes and drain to dry out the greens.

4. Toss the greens with the salad dressing, divide into bowls and serve.

Fantastic Fruity Ice-cream

Preparation Time: *20 Minutes/***Serves:** *6 Servings*

If you can't get your children to eat fruit, hide it in ice cream.

Ingredients

- 4 peeled kiwis
- 600 ml of double cream
- 200 grams of condensed milk
- 3 overly ripe bananas
- The juice of ¼ lemon
- 1 large mango, peeled and seed removed
- 200 grams of hulled strawberries
- Finely chopped mangos and strawberries to serve

Directions

1. Mash the strawberries in a small bowl.

2. Mash the mangos in another small bowl.

3. Combine the banana and lemon juice in a medium sized bow and mash.

4. In a large bowl, combine the cream and the condensed milk and whisk to combine until it becomes stiff and thick.

5. Spoon the mixture into the strawberry, mango, and banana and stir to combine.

6. Transfer the contents of each bowl into three freezer containers and freeze overnight.

7. When ready to serve, slice up the kiwis, divide a scoop of each flavor ice-cream into bowls, top with kiwis and chopped mangos and strawberries and serve.

Spectacular Nut and Fruit Breakfast Bowl

Cooking Time: *10 Minutes/***Serves:** *2 Servings*

Make your oats even more healthy by adding fruits and nuts to them.

Ingredients

- 60 grams of seeds, goji berries, nuts, and pot raisins
- 1 200 ml tub of Greek yogurt
- 2 oranges, peeled, segmented and cut in halves
- 6 tablespoons of porridge oats

Directions

1. Combine the oats and 400 ml of water to a saucepan, cook for 4 minutes over a medium temperature and stir until it thickens.

2. Divide the porridge into bowls, top with yogurt, orange, and nut mixture and serve.

Awesome Avocado and Chicken Spicy Wraps

Cooking Time: *8 Minutes/***Serves**: *2 Servings*

This awesome avocado chicken wrap makes the perfect lunch.

Ingredients

- A few sprigs of chopped coriander
- 1 sliced roasted red pepper
- 1 avocado, stone removed and halved
- 2 seeded wraps
- 1 teaspoon of olive oil
- 1 clove of chopped garlic
- ½ a teaspoon of mild chilli powder
- The juice of ½ a lime
- 1 thinly sliced chicken breast

Directions

1. Combine the chicken, garlic, chilli powder and lime juice in a bowl and stir to combine.

2. Heat the oil in a frying pan over a medium temperature.

3. Fry the chicken for a few minutes, stirring continuously.

4. Heat the wraps according to the directions on the packet.

5. Spread half an avocado onto the wraps.

6. Add the peppers to the frying pan and warm them through.

7. Add the chicken to the wraps, top with the peppers and coriander, roll and serve.

Fabulous Fruit Compote with Red Berry

Cooking Time: *30 Minutes/***Serves:** *6 Servings*

This popular German delight will have you swooning no matter what part of the world you are in.

Ingredients For the Compote

- 500 grams of vanilla custard
- 2 tablespoons of corn starch
- A dash of rosewater
- ½ a tablespoon of golden caster sugar
- ½ a teaspoon of ground cinnamon
- ½ a tablespoon of vanilla extract
- 180 ml of cranberry juice
- 100 grams of mixed strawberries
- 440 grams of canned pitted cherries

Ingredients For the Topping

- 1 handful of mint leaves
- 1 handful of pomegranate seeds
- 1 square of 70% finely grated dark chocolate
- Vanilla custard

Directions

1. Combine the fruits, 150 ml of cranberry juice, rosewater, sugar, cinnamon, and vanilla extract in a large saucepan and cook over medium temperature for 20 minutes until the fruits become soft.

2. In a medium sized bowl, combine the corn starch, and the rest of the cranberry juice and whisk until the mixture is smooth with no lumps.

3. Pour the cranberry juice mixture into the fruit and stir to combine until the ingredients thicken.

4. Put the saucepan to one side and leave the ingredients to cool down.

5. Pour the mixture into a bowl, cover and refrigerate for a minimum of two hours.

6. Serve with vanilla custard, dark chocolate, pomegranate seeds, and mint leaves.

Sultry Seed & Fruit Yogurt

Cooking Time: *5 Minutes/***Serves:** *1 Serving*

This tasty, nutrient-dense fruity snack will keep you going until mealtime.

Ingredients

- 150 gram pot of probiotic yogurt
- ¼ teaspoon of cinnamon
- 1 teaspoon of mixed seeds
- 1 kiwi, sliced

Directions

1. Add the mixed seeds and kiwi to the yogurt, stir to combine and serve.

Ravishing Vanilla Flavored Roasted Fruits

Cooking Time: *20 Minutes/**Serves:** 4 Servings*

Give your fruits an extra spark by roasting them, they taste fabulous with yogurt or ice cream.

Ingredients

- 3 nectarines, sliced into quarters and seeds removed
- 3 peaches, sliced into quarters and seeds removed
- 6 apricots, cut into halves and seeds removed
- The juice of 1 lime
- The zest of 1 lime
- 5 cardamom pods
- 1 split vanilla pod
- 175 grams of golden caster sugar
- Yogurt or ice cream to serve

Directions

1. Prepare the oven by heating it to 350 degrees F.

2. Combine the lime juice, zest, cardamom, vanilla pod, and sugar into a food processor and blend until smooth.

3. Arrange the fruit in a baking dish and top with the sugar mix.

4. Roast the fruits for 20 minutes until they become soft.

5. Once cooked, remove from the oven, and serve with yogurt or ice cream

Perfect Passion Fruit Trifle

Cooking Time: *25 Minutes/***Serves:** *6 Servings*

Add some passion to your dessert with this layered trifle.

Ingredients

- 3 thinly sliced peaches
- 3 thick slices of plain sponge cake
- The juice of 1 orange
- 9 passion fruits cut in halves
- A 300 ml carton of double cream
- 1 teaspoon of vanilla extract
- 50 grams of golden caster sugar
- A 250-gram tub of mascarpone

Directions

1. Combine the vanilla, sugar, and mascarpone's in a large bowl and whisk until smooth.

2. In another large bowl, whisk the double cream until soft peaks are formed.

3. Add the mascarpone mix to the whipped cream, stir to combine, and put it to one side.

4. Scoop the pulp from the passion fruit out into a small bowl, add the orange juice and stir to combine.

5. Arrange the cake in the bottom of a trifle dish.

6. Top with the passion fruit.

7. Top with the peach slices.

8. Finish with a layer of mascarpone.

9. Repeat the process until the ingredients are finished.

10. Put the trifle in the fridge for at least 1 hour and serve.

Conclusion

I hope you've enjoyed these delicious fruit recipes! But most importantly, I hope these dishes have inspired you to start adding more fruit into your diet. There are hundreds of different fruits, and if you want to be a bit more adventurous, you can try using other fruits with these recipes.

I wish you every success on your fruit recipe-making journey!

About the Author

Heston Brown is an accomplished chef and successful e-book author from Palo Alto California. After studying cooking at The New England Culinary Institute, Heston stopped briefly in Chicago where he was offered head chef at some of the city's most prestigious restaurants. Brown decide that he missed the rolling hills and sunny weather of California and moved back to his home state to open up his own catering company and give private cooking classes.

Heston lives in California with his beautiful wife of 18 years and his two daughters who also have aspirations to follow in their father's footsteps and pursue careers in the culinary arts. Brown is well known for his delicious fish and chicken dishes and teaches these recipes as well as many others to his students.

When Heston gave up his successful chef position in Chicago and moved back to California, a friend suggested he use the internet to share his recipes with the world and so he did! To date, Heston Brown has written over 1000 e-books that contain recipes, cooking tips, business strategies for catering companies and a self-help book he wrote from personal experience.

He claims his wife has been his inspiration throughout many of his endeavours and continues to be his partner in business as well as life. His greatest joy is having all three women in his life in the kitchen with him cooking their favourite meal while his favourite jazz music plays in the background.

Author's Afterthoughts

Thank you to all the readers who invested time and money into my book! I cherish every one of you and hope you took the same pleasure in reading it as I did in writing it.

Out of all of the books out there, you chose mine and for that I am truly grateful. It makes the effort worth it when I know my readers are enjoying my work from beginning to end.

Please take a few minutes to write an Amazon review so that others can benefit from your opinions and insight. Your review will help countless other readers make an informed choice

Thank you so much,

Heston Brown

Made in the USA
Monee, IL
12 July 2022

99605506R00052